Samsung Galaxy S25 Ultra 5G User Guide

The Ultimate Tips & Tricks Manual with Simple Instructions and Pictures for Beginners & Advanced User's to Use and Operate the Smartphone

Douglas C. McNally

Copyright © 2025 by Douglas C. McNally

All rights reserved. This book is copyrighted, and no portion of it may be reproduced or transmitted in any form, mechanical, electronic, internet, or otherwise, without permission from the publisher, except in a brief quotation or review of the book.

TABLE OF CONTENTS

INTRODUCTION 1
FUNCTIONS AND LAYOUT OF THE DEVICE . 3
    Hard Buttons 5
    Buttons 5
    Functions 5
        Side Buttons + volume down Buttons 6
        Activating the Side button 6
Battery charging 7
    Charging via Wired 7
    Charging wirelessly 7
    Wireless power sharing 8
SAMSUNG ACCOUNT 10
    Sign out your Samsung account 10
Understanding the Screen 10
Soft-buttons (navigation bar) 13
    Buttons 13
    Function 13
The home screen and the apps screen 14
    Changing between the Apps and Home screens
    14
    Changing the Home screen 15
EDGE PANEL 18
NOTIFICATION PANEL 19

Using the quick settings panel 19
Managing the playback media 21
Screenshot and screen record 21
How to take a screenshot 21
Screen record 23
MAKE USE OF THE KEYBOARD 25
Pasting and copying 27
Extracting text 28
MAKE USE OF THE S PEN 30
Detaching the S Pen 31
Charging the S Pen 31
Enable more than one S Pen 32
Air actions 32
Taking pictures with the S Pen 33
Resetting the S Pen 34
Air command 34
Smart select 36
Taking a video clip of a region 38
Screen write 40
The Bixby Vision 41
Translate 42
PHONE 44
Making phone calls 44
Make an international call 44
Receive Calls 45

Blocking phone numbers 45
CONTACTS 46
  Adding contacts 46
  Importing contacts 46
  Connecting your web accounts and contacts 46
  Looking for contacts 47
    Deleting contacts 48
MESSAGES 48
    Send messages 49
  Reviewing messages 49
CAMERA 51
    Capturing images 51
  Making use of the camera button 52
  Making use of zoom features 53
  Exposure (AE) and focus (AF) locking 54
  Current shooting mode options 54
    In picture mode 58
    Modifying the resolution 58
    Suggestions for shots 58
    Selfie-taking 59
  Capturing crisp close-up images 59
  Using beauty effects and filters 60
  Scanning text or documents 60
  Video mode 61
  Modifying the resolution 62

Video stabilization 62
Using the auto framing feature 63
Dual rec mode 63
Managing the picture-in-picture window while the video is playing 65
Single take mode 66
Portrait mode / Portrait video mode 67
Pro video mode and pro mode 68
Modifying the resolution 69
Keeping the exposure and attention areas apart 69
Night mode 70
Food mode 71
Panorama mode 71
Slow motion Mode 72
Hyperlapse mode 73
GALLERY 74
Viewing pictures 74
Generative edit 75
Image remastering 76
AR ZONE 76
Use the AR Zone 76
Emoji Studio by AR 77
Making an Emoji for AR 77
Choosing which AR emoji to utilize 78
Removing AR Emojis 78

Adding an AR emoji to your contact profile 78
AR Emoji Stickers 79
Making your own stickers 79
Removing stickers with AR emojis 80
Using your AR stickers in conversations 80
AR DOODLE 82
BIXBY 84
Launching Bixby 84
Making use of Bixby 84
Using your voice to wake Bixby 85
BIXBY VISION 85
Making Use of Bixby Vision 86
SAMSUNG INTERNET 88
SAMSUNG WALLET 90
Configuring the Samsung Wallet 90
Make payments 91
Payment cancellation 91
WI-FI 92
Establishing a Wi-Fi network connection 92
Direct Wi-Fi 92
BLUETOOTH 93
CONTACTLESS AND NFC PAYMENTS 94
Using the NFC function to make payments 95
MOBILE HOTSPOT 95

FACIAL RECOGNITION 96
   Add facial recognition 96
   Using your face to unlock the screen 97
   Deleting your registered facial data 97
FINGERPRINT RECOGNITION 98
   Fingerprint registration 98
   Unlock screen with fingerprints 99
   Removing fingerprints that have been registered 99
ABOUT THE AUTHOR 100
INDEX 101

INTRODUCTION

The Galaxy S25 Ultra has undergone significant changes this year, and although many features are unchanged from last year, there are still some fantastic additions. A 50-megapixel ultra-wide camera, a bigger screen, a bespoke Snapdragon 8 Elite for Galaxy CPU, and a plethora of AI technologies are just a few of the improvements.

Despite appearances, the Galaxy S25 Ultra is significantly different from its predecessor thanks to a number of important updates. The most notable change the company has made is the several design adjustments, such as reducing the sharp right angles of earlier Galaxy S flagships and making the edges flat.

The phone's screen size has grown from 6.8 inches to 6.9 inches, thanks to a tiny boost by Samsung. With this redesign, Samsung claims to have been able to cut the bezel by fifteen percent. The smartphone now integrates Proscaler, which is an automatic media upscaler that improves the image quality by forty-three percent.

Another unique change is the upgrade to Gorilla Glass Armor 2. The enhanced durability and improved anti-reflective qualities of this glass make it perfect for high-light settings.

Additionally, the ultra-wide camera lens has been improved to 50 megapixels; thus, enhancing the camera's nighttime performance should improve, and it can double as a macro lens for those breathtakingly close-up shots.

Samsung has embedded the Gen Pro Visual Engine in the camera, driven by artificial intelligence, potentially enhancing photographs taken in a variety of settings by reducing blur and noise. In addition, the camera features simulated aperture adjustments, enabling you to select between f/1.4 and f/14. The company additionally incorporated a spatial temporal filter.

There are a ton of new Galaxy AI functions available on the device, thanks to OneUI 7, which comes preinstalled. The Now Bar, a feature reminiscent of Dynamic Island, displays vital data at the bottom of both the home and lock screens. It is one of the most prominent features. Overviews of the day's events will be provided by Now Brief at various points to help users understand what's happening. There's "ProActive AI," which can help you anticipate and avoid issues like large traffic.

FUNCTIONS AND LAYOUT OF THE DEVICE

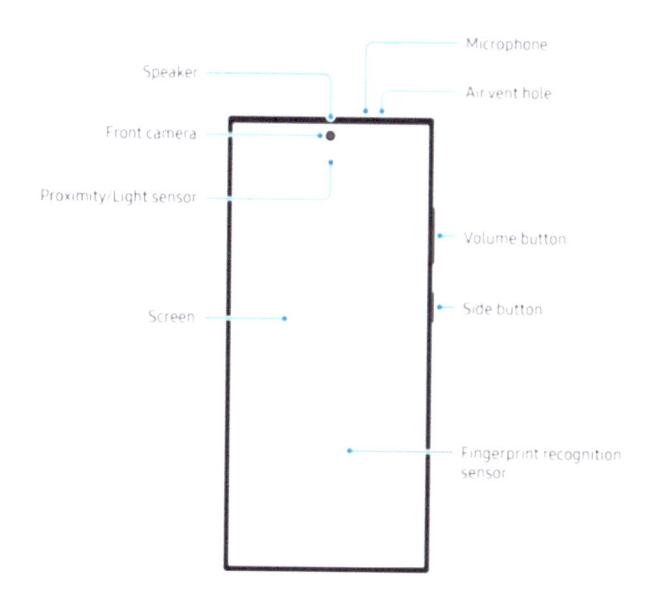

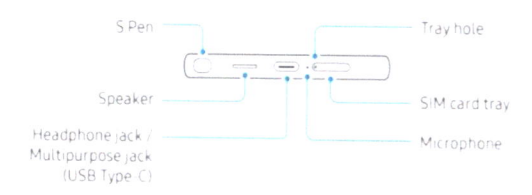

- Microphone
- Speaker
- Air vent hole
- Front camera
- Proximity/Light sensor
- Volume button
- Side button
- Screen
- Fingerprint recognition sensor
- S Pen
- Tray hole
- Speaker
- SIM card tray
- Headphone jack / Multipurpose jack (USB Type-C)
- Microphone

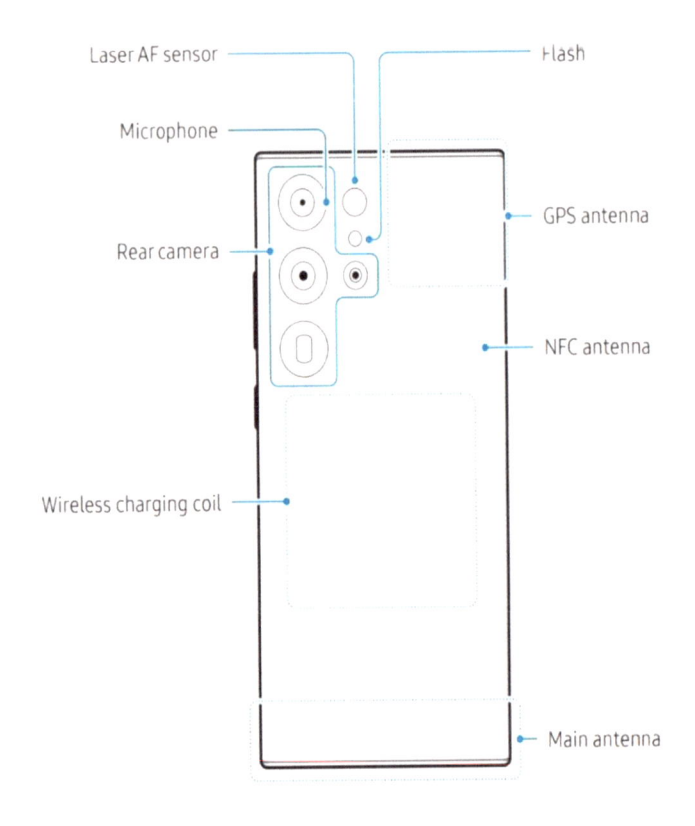

- Laser AF sensor
- Flash
- Microphone
- GPS antenna
- Rear camera
- NFC antenna
- Wireless charging coil
- Main antenna

Hard Buttons

Buttons	Functions
Side Buttons	• To switch the gadget on when it is off, press and hold. • Press to lock the screen or turn it on. • To initiate communication with Bixby, press and hold. For further details, see Using Bixby. • Press and hold or press twice to launch the function or application you've selected.

Side Buttons + volume down Buttons	• To take a screenshot, press all at once.
	• To switch off the device, press and hold at the same time.

Activating the Side button

By tapping the Side button twice or keeping it down, you can choose which app or feature to activate. Select your preferred option after opening Settings and tapping the Advanced features → Side button.

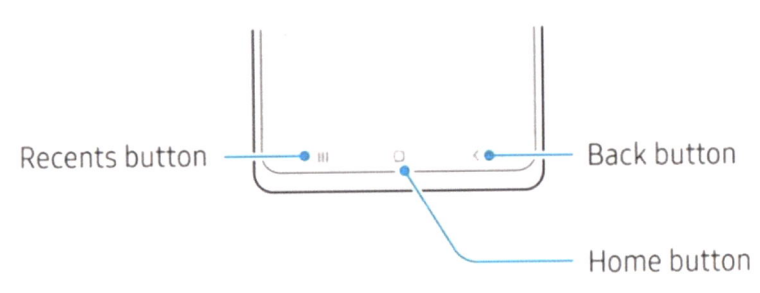

Recents button ——— Back button

——— Home button

The soft buttons will show up at the bottom of the screen when you turn it on. For further details, see the navigation bar (soft buttons).

Battery charging

Before using the battery for the first time or after a prolonged period of inactivity, charge it.

Charging via Wired

To charge the battery, insert the USB cable into the device's multifunctional connector and connect it to the USB power adapter. Disconnect the charger from the gadget once it has finished charging.

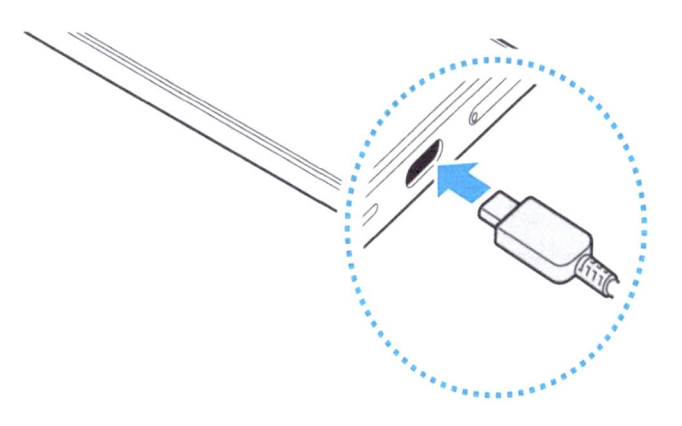

Charging wirelessly

A wireless charging coil is included within the device. A wireless charger, which is available for separate purchase, can be used to charge the battery.

To charge the battery, position the middle of the device's back against the middle of the wireless charger.

Disconnect the gadget from the wireless charger once it has finished charging. The notification panel will provide the expected charging time. The actual charging time may differ based on the charging conditions and is based on the assumption that the device is not in use. Wireless charging may not function properly depending on the kind of cover or accessory. It is advised to remove the cover or accessory from the smartphone in order to achieve reliable wireless charging.

Wireless power sharing

The battery on your phone can be used to charge another gadget. While your phone is charging, you can still charge another device. Wireless power sharing may not function correctly depending on the kind of cover or accessories being used. Before use this feature, it is advised to take off any covers and accessories that are in use.

- To activate wireless power sharing, launch the notification panel, swipe down, and then tap (Wireless power sharing).

Tap ✎ → Edit and drag the button over to add Wireless Power Sharing if you can't locate it on the quick options screen.
- Position the other device, back to front, in the middle of your phone.

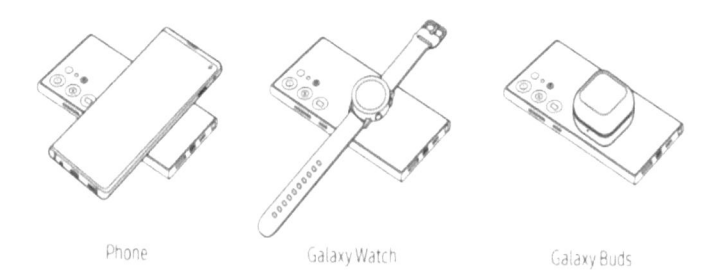

Phone   Galaxy Watch   Galaxy Buds

- Unplug the other item from your phone after charging is complete.

SAMSUNG ACCOUNT

You can access a range of Samsung services via mobile devices, TVs, and the Samsung website by creating an account.

- Launch the Settings app.
- Next, hit **Accounts and backup**.
- Then press **Manage accounts**.
- Here, press **Add account**.
- Finally, hit **Samsung account**.
- Ensure you follow the prompts to insert your details when asked.

Sign out your Samsung account

Contacts, events, and other data will be deleted from your smartphone when you log out of your Samsung account.

- Launch the Settings app.
- Next, hit **Accounts and backup**.
- Then press **Manage accounts**.
- Here, choose the account type.
- Next, select **Remove account**.

Understanding the Screen

Tapping: Press the display.

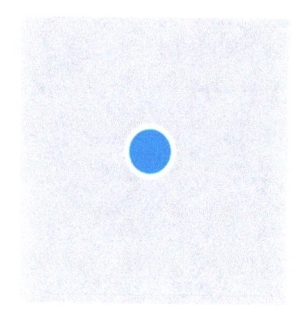

Dragging: Drag an object to the desired location by touching and holding it.

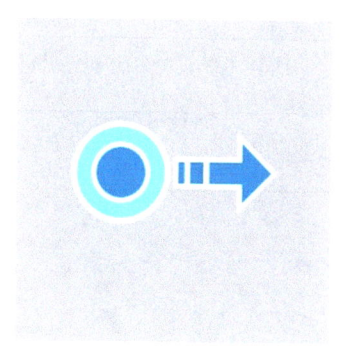

Swiping: You can swipe left, right, upward, or downward.

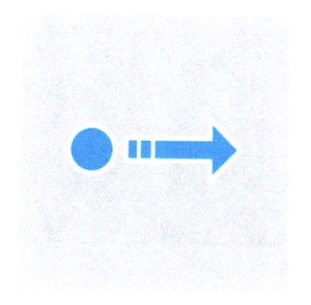

11

Touch and hold: Press and hold the screen for around two seconds.

Double Tap: Tapping the screen twice.

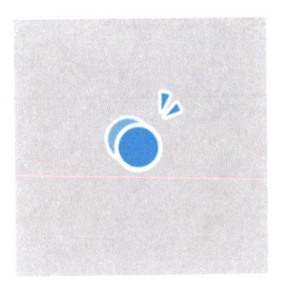

Pinching and spreading: Pinch the screen or spread two fingers apart.

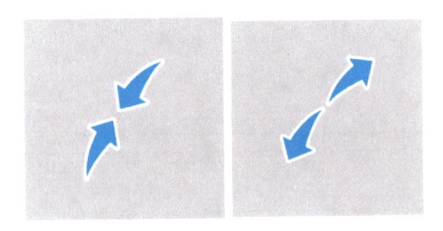

Soft-buttons (navigation bar)

When the screen is turned on, the soft buttons will show up on the bottom navigation bar. By default, the buttons are set to the Recents, Home, and Back buttons; however, their functions can vary depending on the application or environment being used.

Buttons	Function
||| **Recents**	• To view the list of recently installed apps, tap.

Home	• To go back to the Home screen, tap. • To access the search function, touch and hold.
Back	• To go back to the prior screen, tap.

The home screen and the apps screen

All of the device's functionalities can be accessed from the Home screen. Widgets, app shortcuts, and other things are displayed. All apps, even recently installed ones, have icons displayed on the Apps screen.

Changing between the Apps and Home screens

To access the Apps screen from the Home screen, swipe up. Swipe up or down on the Apps screen to go back to the Home screen. As an alternative, press the Back or Home buttons.

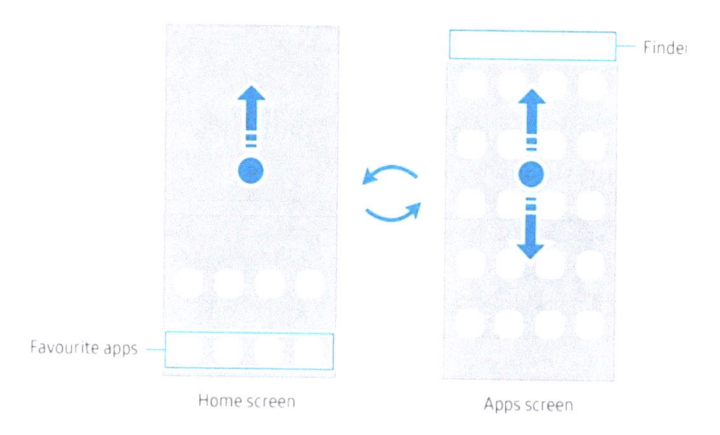

Tapping the Apps button will bring up the Apps screen if it is added to the Home screen. To activate it, touch and hold an empty space on the Home screen, select Settings, and then hit the Home screen switch's Show Apps screen button. At the bottom of the Home screen, there will be an Apps button.

Changing the Home screen

To access the editing options on the Home screen, pinch your fingers together or touch and hold an empty spot. Among other things, you can add widgets and change the background. Home screen panels can also be added, removed, or rearranged.

1. Adding panels: Tap ✚ after swiping to the left.

2. Panel movement: Move a panel preview by dragging it.

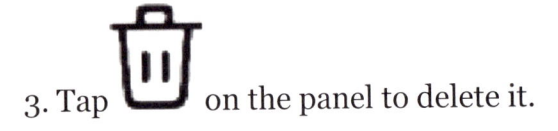

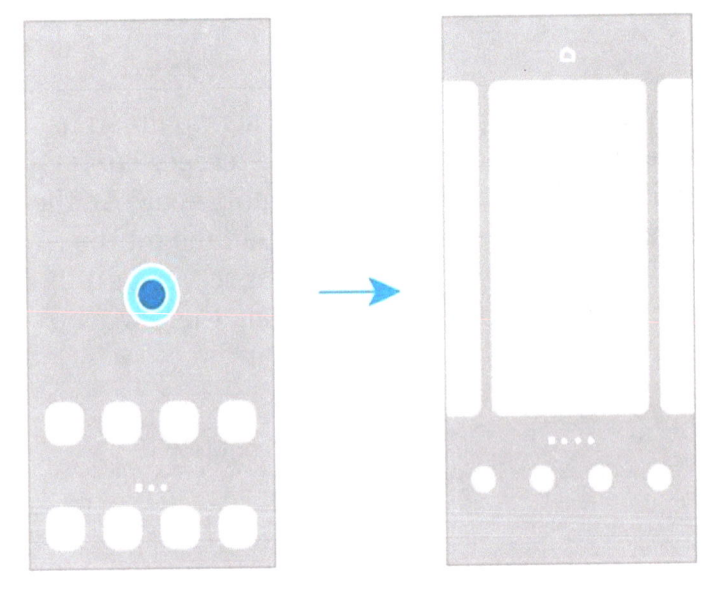

3. Tap 🗑 on the panel to delete it.

- **Wallpapers and Style**: Modify the locked screen's and the Home screen's wallpaper settings.
- **Themes**: Modify the theme of the gadget. The chosen theme will affect the interface's visual components, including colors, icons, and wallpapers.

- **Widgets**: These tiny apps that open particular app features to offer information and easy access on your home screen are known as widgets. After choosing a widget, click **Add**. The Home screen will now have the widget.
- **Options**: Adjust the Home screen's layout and other options.

EDGE PANEL

The Edge panels give you access to your favorite functions and apps. To move the Edge panel handle to the center of the screen, drag it there.

- To enable the Edge panel handle, open Settings app.
- Then, select **Display**.
- Next, press the **Edge panel** option.
- Here, hit the Edge panel switch.

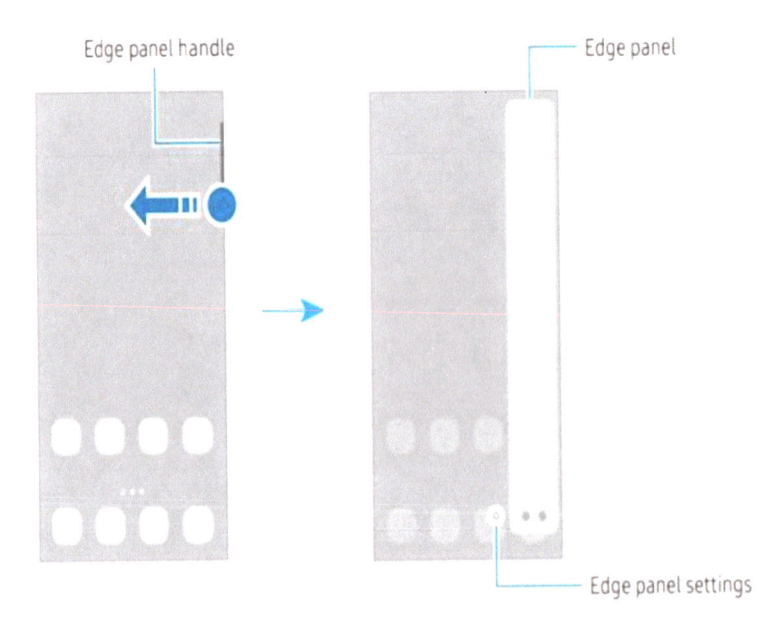

NOTIFICATION PANEL

The status bar displays indicator icons when you get fresh notifications. Open the notification panel and look over the details to see additional facts about the icons. Drag the status bar down to reveal the notification panel. To move away from the notification panel, slide upwards on the screen. The following features are available in the notification panel.

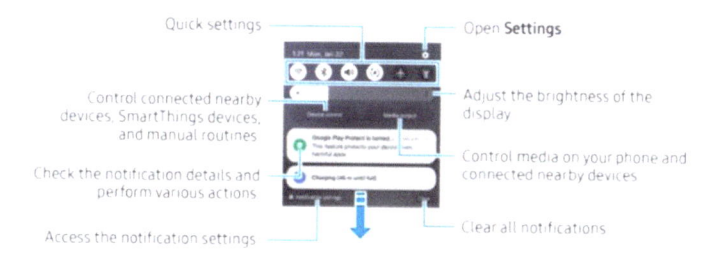

Using the quick settings panel

To access the fast settings panel, swipe down on the notification panel.

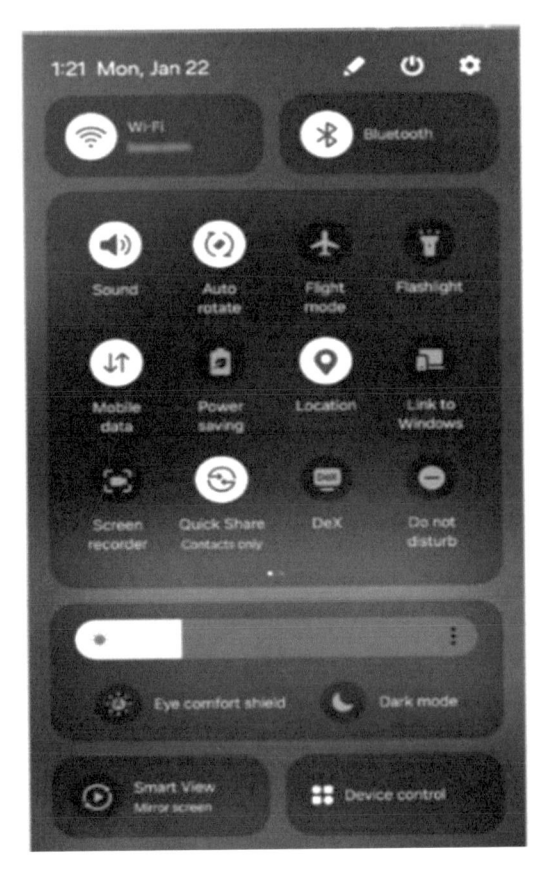

To activate or deactivate a particular feature, tap each button. You can long-tap a button or tap its text to get more extensive options. Tap , then hit **Edit** to edit buttons.

Managing the playback media

Using the notification panel, control the media on your phone and any adjacent devices.

- Tap Media output when the notification panel opens.
- To control the playback, tap the controller's icons.

Screenshot and screen record

While using the device, take a screenshot. Then, you can share, write on, draw on, or crop the screen. Both the scrollable region and the current screen can be captured.

How to take a screenshot

The Gallery is where you may view the screenshots that were taken.

Capturing buttons: At the same time, press the Side and Volume Down buttons.

Swipe capture: Swipe your hand across the screen from left to right using the edge.

- To enable screenshot capture by swiping, go to Settings app.
- Here, select **Advanced features**.
- Then press **Motions & gestures**.
- Inside this menu, select the **Palm swipe to capture** option.
- Hit the switch to activate it.

Some functions and applications do not allow you to take a screenshot. Utilize the choices on the toolbar at the bottom of the screen after taking a screenshot:

- ⟨⟩ : Record both the visible and hidden content on a long page, like a webpage. The screen will automatically scroll down when you tap, capturing additional content.

- ✎ : You can either write or draw on the screenshot or crop a section of it. The clipped section is visible in the Gallery.

- ⌗ : Give the screenshot some tags. Tap and tap the Gallery's search field to find screenshots by tag. You can look for the desired screenshot by accessing the tags list.

- ⤴ : Distribute the screenshot. Open Settings, select **Advanced features**, then press the Screenshots and screen recordings option, and then press the Show toolbar after capturing switch to enable the options if they are not visible on the screen that was taken.

Screen record

While you're using your device, record the screen.

1. To access the screen recorder, open the notification panel, swipe down, and then tap ▣.

2. Tap **Start recording** after choosing a sound setting. The recording will begin following a countdown.

- Tap ✏️ on the screen to write or draw.

- Tap ▼ to bring up the S Pen pointer on the screen. Only when the S Pen is removed from the device can you utilize this feature.

- Tap ⬛ to record the screen with your own video overlay.

MAKE USE OF THE KEYBOARD

By tapping the keyboard icon on the navigation bar, you can switch the text input method. Long-tap the keyboard button on the navigation bar, then choose your preferred option to switch the keyboard button.

- : Voice-enter text. The keyboard should be changed.

- :Open Settings, select **General management** → **Keyboard list** and default, and then tap the keyboard button on the navigation bar switch to activate it if the keyboard button is not visible in the bar.

Other keyboard features:

1. : Add stickers, emojis, and more. Additionally, you can add emoji stickers that resemble you.

25

2. ▣ : Modify the writing style, receive grammar and spelling corrections, and translate messages in specific text messaging and chat applications.

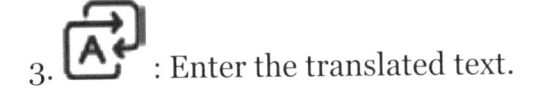

3. ▣ : Enter the translated text.

4. ▣ Take something from the clipboard and add it.

5. ⚙ Modify the keyboard configuration.

••• To access other keyboard operations, tap.

6. ▣ : Change to the handwriting mode.

7. ▭ : Change to the one-handed manner of operation.

8: ▭ : Modify the keyboard setting.

9. 〔T〕 : Identify and input text from papers or pictures.

10. ✚ : Modify the list of keyboard functions. Depending on the model or carrier, certain functionalities might not be accessible.

Pasting and copying
- Touch the text and hold it.
- You can either press choose all to choose all text or drag to select the relevant content.

- Select **Copy** or **Cut**. The clipboard receives a copy of the selected text.
- To input text, touch and hold the desired location, then select Paste. To paste previously copied text, press Clipboard and choose the content.

Extracting text

Some apps, like the Gallery or Camera app, allow you to extract text from photos and use features like sharing or copying. Here are some examples of how to extract text in the Gallery app.

- Tap ⦗T⦘ while viewing a picture in the Gallery app. Only when there is text to extract does the symbol ⦗T⦘ show up.
- Choose a region to extract text from.

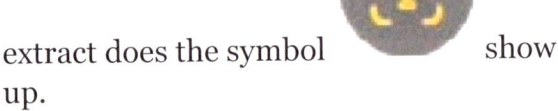

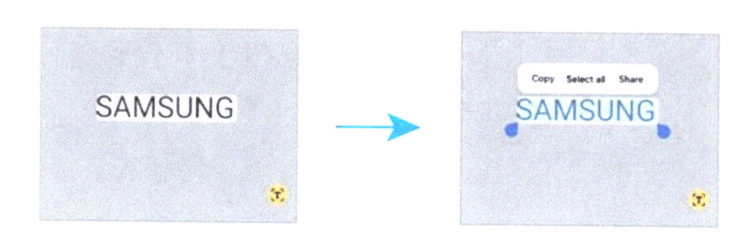

MAKE USE OF THE S PEN

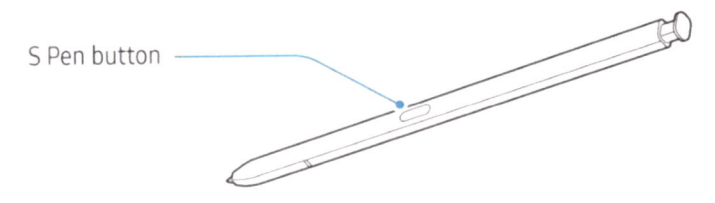

- When using the S Pen, avoid bending it or applying too much pressure. The nib of the S Pen can be distorted or broken.
- Avoid using the S Pen to hard-press the screen. The nib of the pen can be distorted.
- Certain S Pen functions, such charging or screen tapping, might not function if a magnet is present close to the device.
- You can still utilize the S Pen's other features, such tapping the screen or using the Air command features, even if it has been completely charged.
- The device might not recognize the S Pen operations if you use it at sharp angles on the screen.
- Before using the S Pen, drain any water that may have gotten within the slot.
- Take the S Pen to a Samsung service center or an authorized service center if it isn't functioning correctly.

Detaching the S Pen

To disengage the S Pen, press its end. After that, take the S Pen out of the slot. Reposition the S Pen in the slot and press it until it snaps into position to save it.

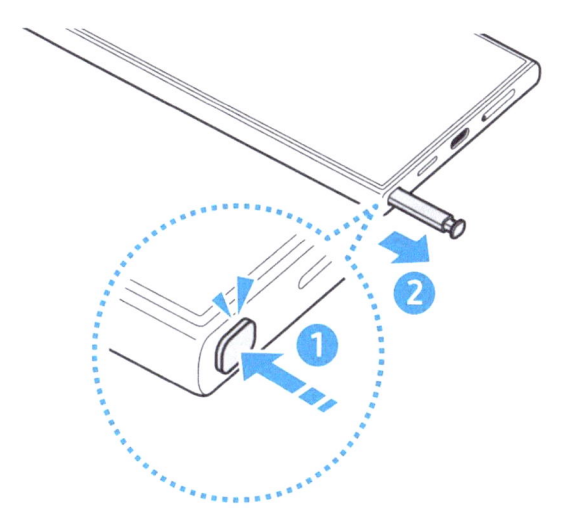

- Open Settings app.
- Next, press **Advanced features**.
- Then select **S Pen**.
- When S Pen is removed, and then choose an option if you want to program an action to run when you remove the S Pen.

Charging the S Pen

Before using the S Pen button to remotely control apps, the pen needs to be charged. Charging will begin as soon as the S Pen is inserted into the slot. The S Pen will only be charged when the device is charging if the Air action function is disabled.

Enable more than one S Pen

- Get to the Settings app.
- Here, select **Advanced features**.
- Next, select **S Pen**.
- Then choose **More S Pen settings**. To activate it, tap the **Allow multiple S Pens** switch.

Air actions

Using the S Pen linked to your device via Bluetooth Low Energy (BLE), you can control apps from a distance. For instance, holding down the S Pen button allows you to launch programs like the camera app. Additionally, you can take a picture with the camera app simply pushing the button once. When music is playing, you can adjust the volume by raising the S Pen while holding down the S Pen button, then lowering it to lower the volume.

- Before using the Air actions function, the S Pen needs to be charged.

- The icon will show up on the status bar as soon as you remove the S Pen from the slot. The S Pen will be detached from the smartphone and the icon will turn grey if it is discharged, too far away, if there are obstructions or outside interference between it and the device. Re-insert the S Pen into the slot to re-connect it to the tablet and utilize the Air actions function.

Taking pictures with the S Pen

Pressing the S Pen button makes it simple to shoot distant pictures without using a timer.

- To activate the feature, open Settings, select **Advanced features**.
- Then choose **S Pen**.
- Next, choose **Air actions**, and then press the switch to activate it if required.
- Navigate to General app actions. Once there, hit the toggle next to Camera to flip it on if required.
- Then select the option next to **Single press**, and select **Take picture**.
- Launch the Camera application.
- To take a picture, press the S Pen button once.
- Holding down the S Pen button allows you to snap a sequence of images.
- Press and hold the S Pen button while moving the pen to the left or right to switch the shooting mode.

- Press the S Pen button twice to switch between cameras.

Resetting the S Pen

Reset the S Pen and reconnect it if there are issues with the connection or if it disconnects frequently.

- Slide the S Pen into the opening.
- Get to the Settings app.
- Next, select **Advanced features**.
- Then select **S Pen**.

- Press the triple dots at the top ⋮ .
- Then press **Reset S Pen**.

Air command

Air command is a menu that offers immediate access to commonly used apps and S Pen functionality. To access the Air command panel and choose a desired function or application, tap the Air command icon with the S Pen. Hovering the S Pen over the Air command icon allows you to view the actions that are accessible in each app that supports the Air actions feature. Drag to a new spot to relocate the Air command icon ![pen icon]. Drag to Remove at the bottom of the screen to get rid of the icon ![pen icon]. Open Settings, select **Advanced features**, then select **S Pen** and press **Air command**, and then press the Show Air command icon option to enable the Air command icon ![pen icon] if it is not visible on the screen. Hovering the S Pen over the screen and hitting the S Pen button will open the Air command panel if the Open Air command with Pen button switch is enabled.

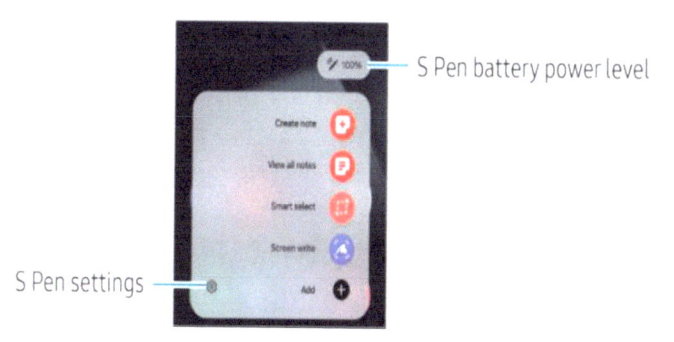

S Pen battery power level

S Pen settings

- Create note: Use a pop-up window to create notes. Double touching the screen while holding down the S Pen button is another way to activate this feature. For further details, see Samsung Notes.
- See every note: Use the Samsung Notes app to view all of your notes.

- Smart select: Choose an area and carry out operations, such sharing or storing, with the S Pen. For further details, see Smart Select.
- Screen write: Take screenshots and crop a portion of the image or write or draw on them. On a large page, like a webpage, you can also record both the visible and buried text. For further details, see Screen write.
- Bixby Vision: Make use of Bixby Vision's capabilities to translate text, find related photos, and more. For more details, see Bixby Vision.
- Translate: To translate a word, move the S Pen over it. For additional details, see Translate.
- Magnify: To make a section of the screen larger, move the S Pen over it.
- PENUP: Share your artwork, view the work of others, and receive helpful drawing advice. Open the Calendar app, then write or draw on the screen. For further details, see Write on Calendar.
- Add: Give the Air command panel shortcuts to commonly used programs.

Smart select

To choose an area and carry out operations, such sharing or saving, use the S Pen.

You can pick a segment of a video and save it as a GIF. One To capture specific content, such a portion of an image, open the Air command panel and pick Smart.

1. Drag the S Pen across the content you wish to choose after selecting a preferred shape icon from the toolbar.

2. Choose an option to apply to the chosen region.

• Pin: Attach the chosen region to the screen with a pin. The picture can easily be added to other apps, such Samsung Notes. Drag the picture to the screen of the other application.

• Copy: Take the chosen portion and paste it into another application or other devices that are logged into your Samsung account.

• ⬚ : Take text out of the chosen area.

• ⬚ : Modifies the chosen area's look automatically.

- ![icon] :On the chosen area, write or draw.

- ![icon] : Let people know about the chosen place.

- ![icon] : Save the chosen region in the Gallery.

Taking a video clip of a region

Choose a section of a video and record it as a GIF.

1. Open the Air command panel and select Smart select if you wish to record video while it's playing.

2. Tap ![GIF icon] on the toolbar.

3 Modify the capturing area's size and location.

4. To begin recording, tap Record.

- Verify that the video is playing before taking a picture.
- The screen will indicate the longest you can record a segment of the video for.

- Sound will not be captured while capturing a section of a video.

5. To stop capturing, tap Stop.

6. Choose an option to apply to the chosen location.

- Pin: Attach the chosen region to the screen with a pin. The GIF can also be added to other applications, such Samsung Notes. Drag the GIF to the screen of the other application.
- Copy: Select the region you want to copy and paste into another app or other devices that are logged into your Samsung account.

- ![icon] :On the chosen area, write or draw.

Before saving the file, tap ![play] to see the outcome.

- ![share] : Let people know about the chosen place.

- ![save] : Save the chosen region in the Gallery.

Screen write

Take screenshots so you may write, draw, or crop a portion of the image.

1. Tap Screen write in the Air command panel after selecting the content you wish to record.

The editing toolbar opens and the current screen is automatically captured.

2. On the screenshot, write a memo.

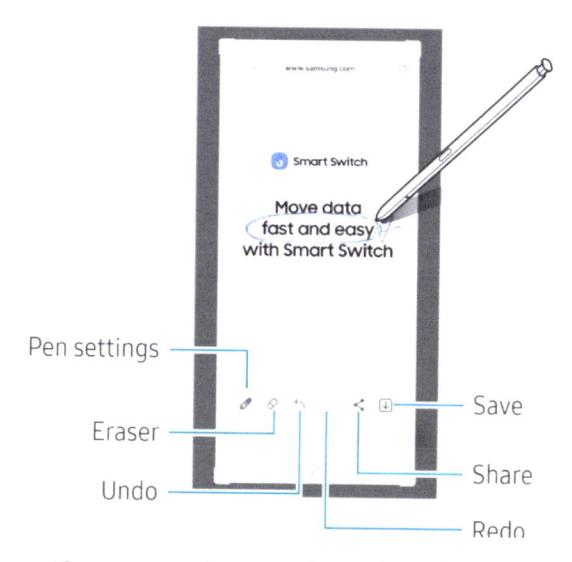

Pen settings

Eraser

Undo

Save

Share

Redo

3. Save the screenshot or share it. The screenshots that were taken can be viewed in the Gallery. Some programs do not allow you to take a screenshot while using them.

The Bixby Vision

Hovering the S Pen over the material identifies it and displays the available search icons. Utilize the tools to find related images, identify and translate text, and more. For more details, see Bixby Vision.

1. To search for pertinent information or extract text from an image, open the Air command panel and select Bixby Vision.

2. Move the S Pen pointer over the desired information. Choose your preferred option when the available alternatives show up on the screen.

Translate

To translate a text, move the S Pen over it. Additionally, the text's units will be transformed.

1. To translate text, enter the Air command panel and select the "**Translate**" option.

2. On the translator panel at the top of the screen, choose the languages you want to use. By

touching ⊡ or ⊟, you can switch between words and sentences.

3. To convert a unit or translate text, move the S Pen over the desired text. The translated text will show up. Press 🔊 to hear how the original text is pronounced. Depending on the language you choose, the 🔊 icon might not show up.

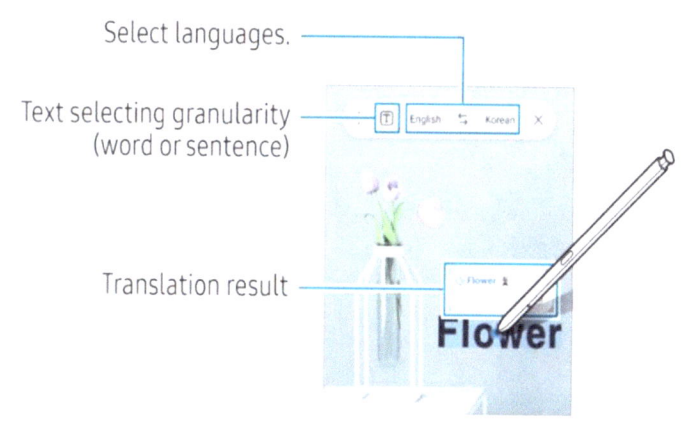

Select languages.

Text selecting granularity (word or sentence)

Translation result

- Some languages are not supported by this functionality.
- Only when there is detectable text on the screen is this feature accessible.

43

PIIONE

Make and receive video and audio calls.

Making phone calls

1. Launch the Phone app, then choose Keypad.

2. Type a phone number in here.

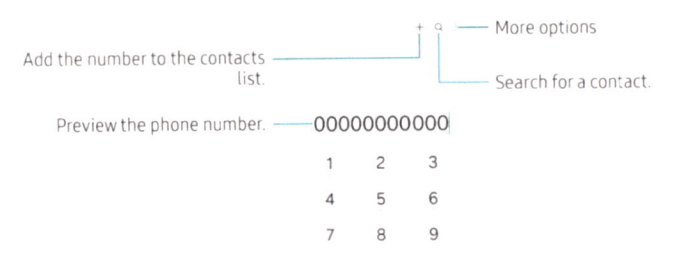

3. You can tap ▢ to make a video call or a voice call ☎ .

```
                                          + ⌕  ── More options
Add the number to the contacts ────┐  │
                         list.        └── Search for a contact.
   Preview the phone number. ── 00000000000
                               1   2   3
                               4   5   6
                               7   8   9
```

Make an international call

1. Launch the Phone app, then choose Keypad.

2. Press and hold 0 to bring up the + symbol.

3. Tap after entering the phone number, area code, and country code.

Receive Calls

- Taking a call: Drag outside the big circle when someone calls.

- Turning down a call: Drag outside the big circle when someone calls. Drag the

Blocking phone numbers

Stop calls from particular numbers that have been added to your block list. Select contacts or phone numbers to add to the prohibited numbers list after opening the Phone app and tapping ● → **Settings** → **Block numbers**. You won't be notified when blocked numbers attempt to reach you. The call log will contain the call log entries. Incoming calls from those who fail to display their caller ID can also be blocked. Turn on the feature by tapping the switch labeled "Block calls from unknown numbers."

CONTACTS

Adding contacts

1. Launch the Contacts app, then press ➕.

2. Decide on a place for storage.

3. After entering your contact details, click **Save**.

Importing contacts

You can add contacts to your device by importing them from other storage devices. 1. Tap ☰ → Manage contacts → Import contacts after launching the Contacts app.

2. To import contacts, adhere to the on-screen directions.

Connecting your web accounts and contacts

Sync the contacts on your device with those stored online in your web accounts, like your Samsung account.

1. Select the account to sync with by opening Settings, tapping Accounts and backup, then choosing Manage accounts.

2. To activate it, press the Contacts switch after selecting Sync account.

Looking for contacts

Launch the Contacts application. Enter search parameters by tapping at the top of the contacts list. Give the contact a tap. After that, do one of the following:

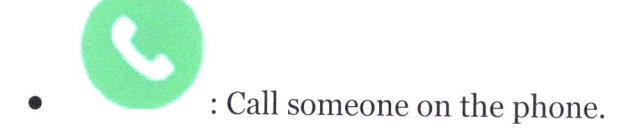

- 📞 : Call someone on the phone.

- 💬 Write a message.

- 📹 : Write an email.

- 🎥 : Make a video call.

- ✉ : Write an email.

Deleting contacts

1. Tap ⋮ → Edit after launching the Contacts app.

2. Tap **Delete** after selecting contacts. Select a contact from the contacts list, then select More → Delete to remove each contact individually.

MESSAGES

Messages can be sent and checked by discussion. Additional fees could apply if you send or receive messages when you are

Send messages

1. Launch the Messages app, then press ![icon].

2. Type a message and add recipients. Touch and hold, then speak your message to record and send a voice message. Only when the message input field is empty does the recording icon show up.

3. Tap ![icon] to send the message.

Reviewing messages

1. Tap ![+] Conversations after launching the Messages app.

2. Choose a phone number or contact from the messages list.

- Tap the message input field, type a message, and then tap to respond to the message.
- You can pinch the screen or spread two fingers apart to change the font size.

- Message sorting Messages can be sorted by category. Tap Conversations ● → after launching the Messages app. To enable the category option if it isn't there, go to Settings and press the Conversation categories switch.
- Removing messages To remove a message, touch and hold it, then select Delete.

CAMERA

Use a variety of settings and modes to take photos and capture videos.

Capturing images
- Launch the Camera application. Alternatively, you can drag to the left on the locked screen or press the Side button twice to launch the app.
- While you launch the Camera app from a locked screen or while the screen is off and the screen lock mechanism is enabled, certain camera capabilities are not accessible.
- Wherever the camera should focus, tap the image on the preview screen. Drag the adjustment bar that shows up above or below the circular frame to change the brightness of images.

- To snap a photo, tap ◯. Drag the list of shooting modes to the left or right, or swipe left or right on the preview screen, to switch the shooting mode.

Camera settings — Options for current shooting mode

Zoom

Shooting modes list

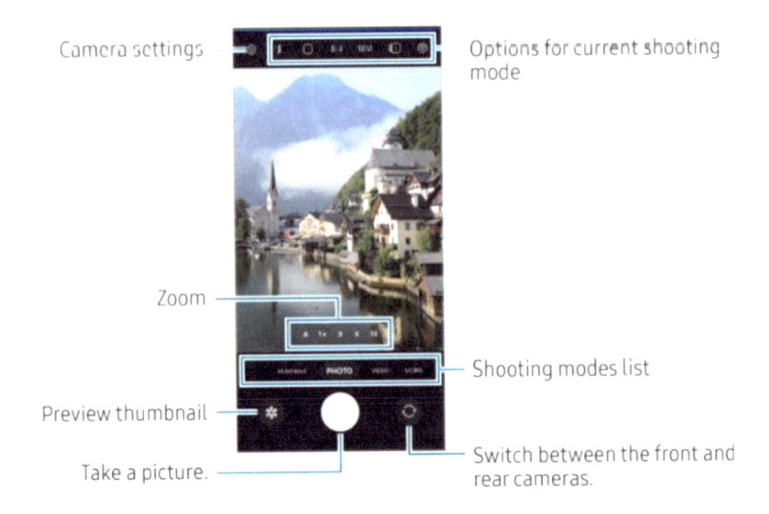

Preview thumbnail

Take a picture. — Switch between the front and rear cameras.

- Depending on the camera being used and the shooting mode, the preview screen may change.

Making use of the camera button

- To capture a video, press and hold the camera button.
- You can record a video without holding down the camera button if you move it to the symbol ![lock icon].
- Swipe the camera button to the screen's edge and keep it there to capture quick images. You may make GIFs by tapping

⚙️ on the preview screen and then selecting the Swipe Shutter button to → Create GIF.
- You can take images more easily and move the camera button anywhere on the screen if you add another one. To activate it, hit the Floating Shutter button option on the preview screen after selecting ⚙️ → Shooting methods.

Making use of zoom features

Choose the preferred zoom icon on the preview screen to zoom in or out while using the rear camera.

When you tap the zoom icon, a list of zoom levels shows, from which you can choose the required zoom level. You can squeeze, split two fingers apart, or drag the zoom icon on the preview screen to fine-tune the zoom. A zoom guide map will show where you are zooming in on the image if the zoom ratio rises beyond a predetermined threshold.

Zoom guide map

Zoom

Zoom level list

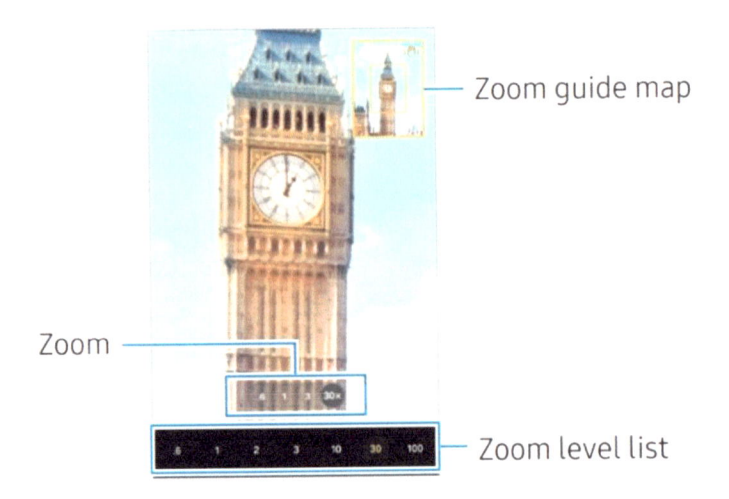

Exposure (AE) and focus (AF) locking

To stop the camera from changing itself in response to changes in the subject or light sources, you can lock the focus or exposure on a specific region. To focus, touch and hold the spot. The focus and exposure settings will be locked, and the AF/AE frame will show up on the scene. Even after you take a picture, the setting stays locked.

Current shooting mode options

Use the choices below on the preview screen.

- ⚡: Activate or deactivate the flash.

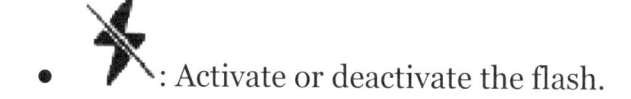

- 🕐: Choose how long to wait before the camera snaps a picture on its own.

- **3:4**: Choose a picture aspect ratio.

- **12M**: Choose a photo resolution.

- ▶: Activate or deactivate the motion photo function. A video clip will also be recorded from a few seconds prior to pressing the camera button if you enable it.

- 🏃: Activate or deactivate the extremely steady feature.

- ⏲∞: Modify the time when hyperlapse videos are recorded. • AUTO:

For hyperlapse videos, choose a frame rate.

- **9:16**: Choose a video aspect ratio.

- **FHD 30** / **FHD** : Choose a video resolution.

- ![icon]: Use a beauty effect or filter effect. Choose a metering technique.

- ![icon]: The calculation of light values is based on this. Center-weighted metering determines the exposure of the shot by measuring the light in the middle of the image.

- ![icon]: The entire scene is averaged using matrix metering ![icon]. Spot metering ![icon] determines the exposure of the

56

shot by measuring the light in a concentrated central region.

- ⊚ : Modify the color scheme.

- 💧 : When in **FOOD** mode, blur the image outside the frame while focusing on an object inside.

- 🌡 : Modify the color temperature in FOOD mode.

- ⤓ : Modify the saving setting in **DUAL REC** mode.

- ▣ : Switch the screen while in **DUAL REC** mode.

- ⇄ : When capturing single-take photos, adjust the shooting parameters.

57

In picture mode
Depending on the situation, the camera automatically modifies the shooting settings. To take a picture, hit **PHOTO** and hit ◯ from the list of shooting options.

Modifying the resolution
You are able to capture high-quality images. Select the desired resolution by tapping **12M** in the shooting settings, then snap a photo. The model may have a different resolution.

Suggestions for shots
The camera uses the subject's position and angle to determine the best composition for the image. To activate Shot recommendations, repeatedly tap the switch on the preview screen.

1 Select **PHOTO** from the list of shooting modes. The preview screen will show a guide.

2 Aim the guide directly at the topic. The suggested composition shows up on the preview screen after the camera detects it.

3. Adjust the gadget so that the composition suggested by the guidance is followed. The

guidance will turn yellow once the composition is perfect.

4. To snap a photo, tap ◯.

Selfie-taking

The front camera can be used to capture self-portraits.

1. To switch to the front camera for self-portraits, tap ⟳ or swipe up or down on the preview screen.

2. Turn to face the camera's front lens. Tap to capture self-portraits of individuals or landscapes from a wide angle.

3 To snap a photo, tap ◯.

Capturing crisp close-up images

- Take crisp, up-close photos of your subject.
- Tap **1×** on the preview screen.
- Position the lens close to the topic.

- To take a picture, tap ⦿ when it appears. Tap ◯ to activate this feature if it isn't already enabled.

Using beauty effects and filters
Before snapping a photo, you can choose a filter effect and adjust your face's shape and skin tone.

- Tap ◈ on the preview screen.
- Choose effects and snap a photo. By tapping ⊕, you may either download filters or make your own by selecting a picture from the Gallery with a desired color tone.

Scanning text or documents
Text or documents can be scanned.

- Select **PHOTO** from the list of shooting modes.
- 2. Tap ⊙ the object while pointing the camera in its direction. Only when a document or text is detected will the symbol ⊙ show up.
- After choosing the desired area by tapping **Scan**, touch **Save**.

Video mode

Depending on the situation, the camera automatically modifies the shooting settings.

- To record a video ⬤ , select **VIDEO** from the list of shooting modes.
- During recording, you may press or swipe up or down on the preview screen ⊙ to switch between the front and rear cameras.
- Tap ⊙ to take a picture of the video as its being recorded.

- When shooting a video, point the camera in that direction and adjust the zoom to record the sound from that direction at a higher level.

- To end the video recording, tap ▇.
- To save your device from overheating, the video quality may decrease if you utilize the video zoom feature for an extended period of time while recording.
- In low light conditions, the optical zoom might not function.

Modifying the resolution

A maximum resolution of 8K is available for high-quality video recording. Tap to select the desired resolution under the shooting settings, then record a video. Play the video in the Gallery app after you've finished recording it. A photo of the frame will be saved when you tap on one that you like.

Video stabilization

Use the Super steady function to further stabilize videos if there is a lot of shake when filming. To activate shooting, press the shooting options

, then select VIDEO from the list of shooting modes. Next, record a video.

Using the auto framing feature

By identifying and tracking individuals during video recording, you can configure the device to automatically adjust the zoom and shooting angle. Select **VIDEO** from the list of shooting modes, tap   to activate it, and then record a video. Tap the frame that appears around the subject to track them, change the camera angle, and zoom in on them. Tap the frame once more to stop tracking.

Dual rec mode

Use two cameras to simultaneously record videos. Each camera's video can be edited and saved independently. Additionally, there are other methods to play the videos, including picture-in-picture and split view.

- Tap **MORE**, then select **DUAL REC** from the list of shooting modes.

- Press ⊞, choose two lenses, then press **OK**.

- Tap ⤓ to store each camera's video separately.

- Tap ⧈ to switch the screen.

- To record a video, tap ⏺.

- To end the video recording, tap ■.

Change the saving option.

Change the screen

Picture-in-picture window

Managing the picture-in-picture window while the video is playing

- While recording or watching a video, you can adjust the ▣ picture-in-picture window's size or position if you have the screen in picture-in-picture view.

- To switch the saving option ⬇ to Save videos in individual files, tap ⬇ on the preview screen.

- To record a video, tap ●. Before and during recording, you can adjust the picture-in-picture window's size and position.

- Tap ⛶ the window repeatedly to make the picture-in-picture window larger.

- Drag the picture-in-picture window to the desired location.

- To end the video recording, tap ■. While the video is playing, you can also manipulate the picture-in-picture

window. Either launch the Gallery app,
pick the video, and then tap ⋮ →
launch in Video player, or tap the preview
thumbnail on the preview screen.

Single take mode

Capture many images and movies in a single shot. The best shot is automatically chosen by your device, which then produces films with certain parts repeated or images with filters.

- Select **MORE** → **SINGLE TAKE** from the list of shooting modes.
- Tap ◯ to record the desired scene.
- Either launch the Gallery app and choose the file, or tap the preview thumbnail on the preview screen. Tap the icon to view additional results. Touch and hold an item, check the items you want, and then press ⬇ to save each result separately.

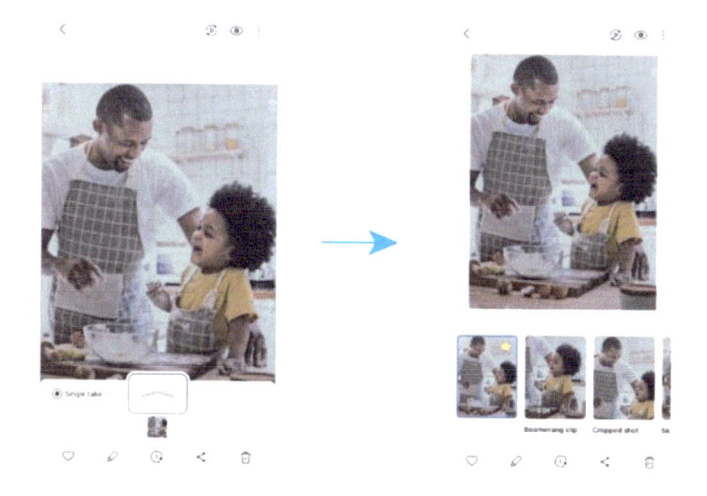

Portrait mode / Portrait video mode

You can take images or films where the subject is clearly seen and the surrounding is blurred by utilizing the Portrait mode or Portrait video mode. After shooting a photo, you can also edit it and apply a backdrop effect.

- Select **PORTRAIT** or **MORE → PORTRAIT VIDEO** from the list of shooting modes.

- Tap and choose your preferred background effect. Drag the adjustment bar to change the background effect's intensity.

- Tap ⏺ to record a video or tap ⭕ to take a picture when the preview screen says "**Ready**."

Background effect intensity adjustment bar — Background effects

- Depending on the shooting mode, several options might be offered.
- Make use of this feature in an area with enough light.
- If the subject is thin or transparent, or if the device or subject is moving, the background blur may not be applied correctly. The topic and background are both plain, and their colors are identical.

Pro video mode and pro mode

Take images or videos while manually modifying the exposure and ISO values, among other shooting parameters.

- Tap **MORE** → **PRO** or **PRO VIDEO** from the list of shooting modes.

- After choosing options and adjusting the settings, press 🔴 to record a video or ⭕ capture a picture.

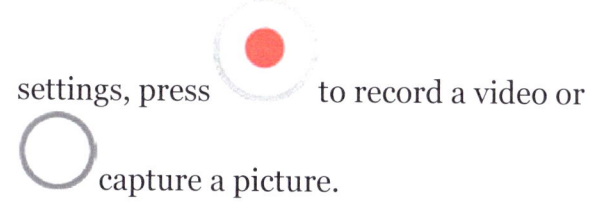

Modifying the resolution

A maximum resolution of 8K is available for high-quality video recording.

Tap **FHD 30** to select the desired resolution under the shooting settings, then record a video. Play the video in the Gallery app after you've finished recording it. A photo of the frame will be saved when you tap ▶ on one that you like.

Keeping the exposure and attention areas apart

The exposure area and the focal area are separable. You can touch the preview screen to lock the focus area and hold it there until the AF/AE lock frame shows up. It will then split into AF lock and AE lock frames before joining back to the AF/AE lock frame. To make the exposure area lock, tap once more and move the AE lock frame to the desired spot.

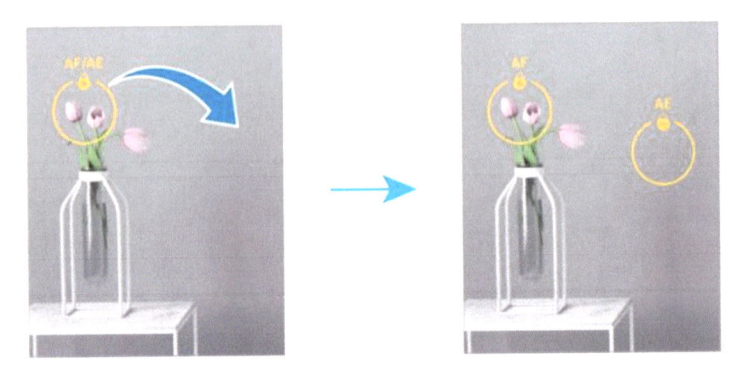

Night mode
Without utilizing the flash, take a photo in low light. Results can be more stable and brighter if you use a tripod.

- Select **MORE** → **NIGHT** from the list of shooting modes. You can obtain crisper images if you set the time that shows at the bottom right of the screen to Max.
- Hold your cellphone steady while tapping ○ to finish shooting.

Food mode

Photograph food that has bright colors and hazy edges.

- Select **MORE → FOOD** from the list of shooting modes. The region outside the frame will be blurred when a frame appears on the screen.
- Drag a corner of the frame to change its size. To move the frame, drag it or tap the desired location.
- To change the color temperature, tap 🌡 and drag the adjustment bar.
- To snap a photo, tap ◯.

Panorama mode

Take a number of photos in panorama mode, then combine them to form a broad scene.

- Select **MORE → PANORAMA** from the list of shooting modes.
- Slowly move the gadget in one way while tapping ◯. Keep the picture in the viewfinder of the camera. The device will automatically stop taking images if the preview image is outside of the guiding frame or if you don't adjust it.

- To stop snapping photos, tap ■.
  Steer clear of photographing blurry backdrops like a blank sky or a plain wall.

Slow motion Mode

Make a video to watch in slow motion. You can designate which parts of your videos will play slowly.

- To record a video press ⦿, press **MORE → SLOW MOTION** on the list of shooting options.

- Tap ■ to end recording when you're done.

- Tap the preview thumbnail on the preview screen. After setting the quick portion of the video to slow motion, the video will begin to play. Based on the footage, up to two slow motion segments will be produced. Tap ✎ and drag the section editing bar to the left or right to make changes to the slow motion portion.

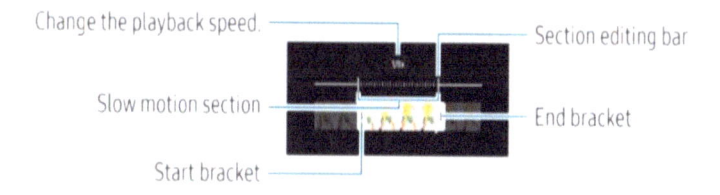

Change the playback speed.
Section editing bar
Slow motion section
End bracket
Start bracket

Hyperlapse mode

Take pictures of scenes, like passing vehicles or people, then watch them as fast-motion films.

- Select **MORE → HYPERLAPSE** from the list of shooting modes.
- Choose a frame rate by tapping **AUTO**.
- The gadget will automatically alter the frame rate based on the scene's changing rate if you set it to **AUTO**.
- Tap to choose the frame rate if you wish to record star trails.

- To begin recording, tap ⬤.

- To complete the recording, tap ■.

73

GALLERY

View the pictures and movies that are saved on your device. Additionally, you can make stories or organize photos and videos by album.

Launch the Gallery application.

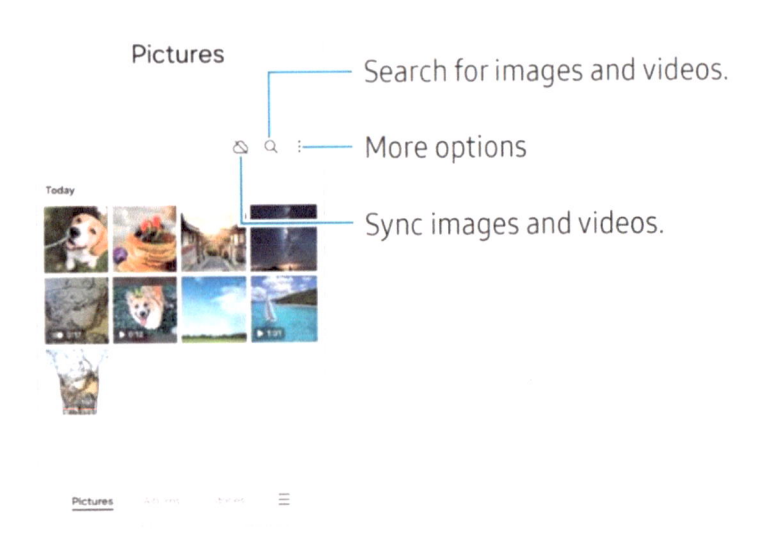

Viewing pictures

Launch the Gallery app, then pick a picture.
Swipe left or right on the screen to browse other files.

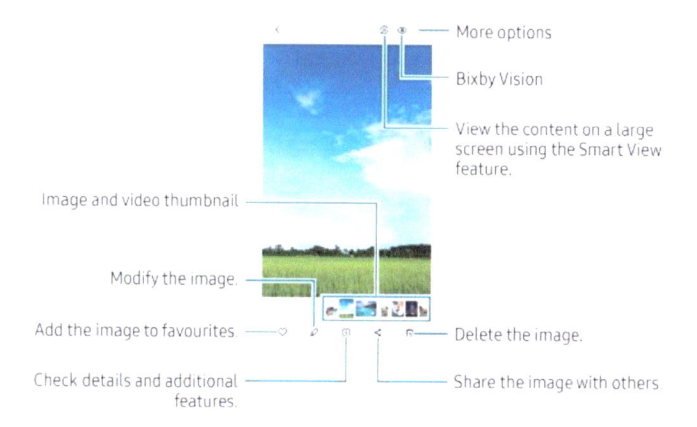

Generative edit

To fill in any gaps, create a new background after editing photos by resizing, moving, or eliminating people or objects.

- Choose an image by opening the Gallery app.
- Click ✏️ Press → ✨ .
- To move or remove anything, tap or draw around it. You may move the tilt adjustment bar to change the tilt.
- You can either tap to remove the selected region or touch and hold it to move it to the desired location.
- Press "**Generate**."
- To save the picture, tap **Done**.

75

Image remastering

Low-resolution, grainy, and boring photos can be improved.

- Choose an image by opening the Gallery app.
- Tap the triple dots icon.
- Next, select the **Remaster picture** option. The before and after can be seen.
- Tap ⬇ to save it.

AR ZONE

You may get AR-related features from AR Zone. Select a feature and record entertaining images or movies.

Use the AR Zone

To start AR Zone, use the following techniques:

- Select **AR ZONE** from the list of shooting modes in the Camera app by tapping **MORE**.

- Launch the AR Zone app if you added the app icon to the Apps screen. Depending on the model or carrier, certain functionalities might not be accessible.

Emoji Studio by AR

Make emoji's whatever you choose, then enjoy using them in different contexts.

Making an Emoji for AR
- Tap AR Emoji Studio after launching AR Zone.
- Choose from a variety of pre-made emojis. Choose an emoji by swiping left or right, then tapping →.
- Take a selfie or choose a picture to create your own emoji.

Choosing which AR emoji to utilize

Choose your preferred emoji by tapping ⚙ on it on the main screen of AR Emoji Studio.

Removing AR Emojis

Touch ⚙ on the main panel of AR Emoji Studio, select which emojis to remove, and then touch Delete 🗑.

Adding an AR emoji to your contact profile

In the Contacts app and on your Samsung account, set an emoji as your profile image. You can make your own expressions or select from a variety of stances.

- Select an emoji by tapping Profile on the main page of AR Emoji Studio.

- Tap ○ to choose a desired stance or to record your expression.

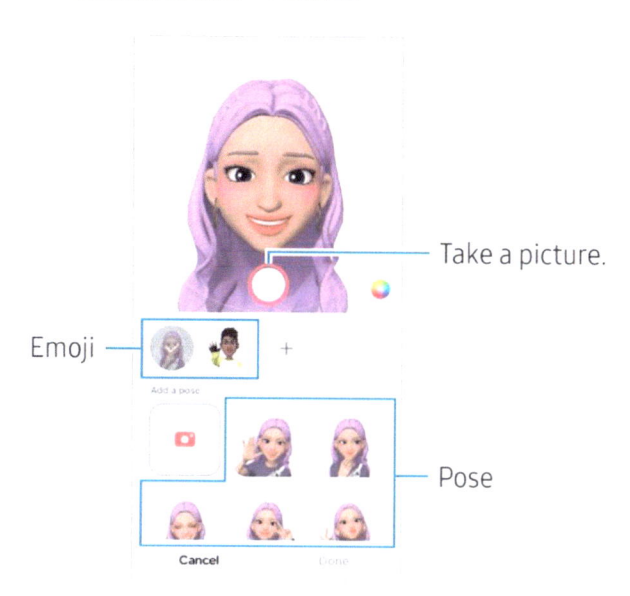

- Select Done → Save.

AR Emoji Stickers
Stickers with emoji actions and expressions will be generated automatically when you create AR emojis. By altering the backdrop or emotion, you may even make your own stickers. You can use your emoji stickers on social media or when sending communications.

Making your own stickers
- Tap AR Emoji Stickers after launching AR Zone.

- Tap ➕ at the sticker list's top.
- Modify stickers as you see fit, then click Save. At the top of the stickers list, you can see the stickers you have made.

Removing stickers with AR emojis

Select AR Emoji Stickers → ⋮ → Edit after launching AR Zone. Tap Delete after selecting the emoji stickers to remove.

Using your AR stickers in conversations

You can use your emoji stickers on social media or in mails while having a conversation. Here are some examples of how to use your emoji stickers in the Messages app.

- Tap 🙂 on the Samsung Keyboard when writing a message in the Messages app.
- Press the emoji symbol 🙂.
- Choose an emoji sticker from your collection. We'll insert the emoji sticker.

Emoji icon

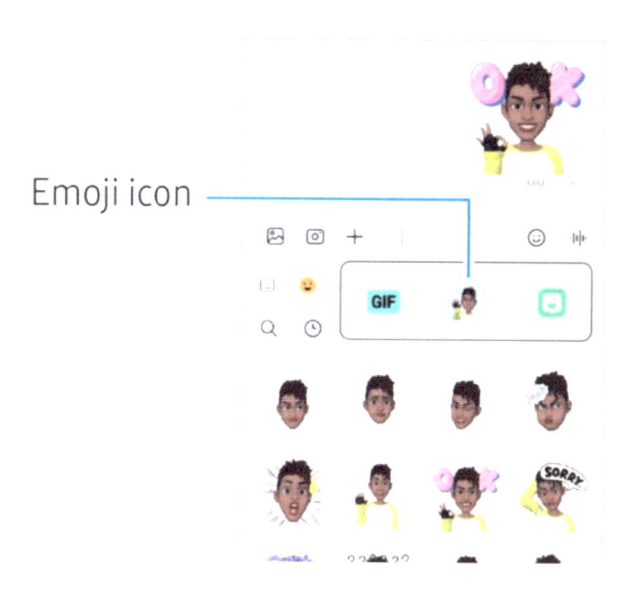

AR DOODLE

Make entertaining videos with drawings or virtual handwriting on the faces of people, animals (dogs and cats), or other objects. The drawings on a face will follow the face as it moves when the camera detects it, and the doodles in the area will remain fixed in place even if the camera moves.

- Tap AR Doodle after launching AR Zone. The recognition area will show up on the screen once the camera has identified the subject.
- In the recognition box, write or draw.
- You can also write or draw outside the recognition area if you use the rear camera.
- You can record yourself doodling if you tap ⏺ and start drawing.

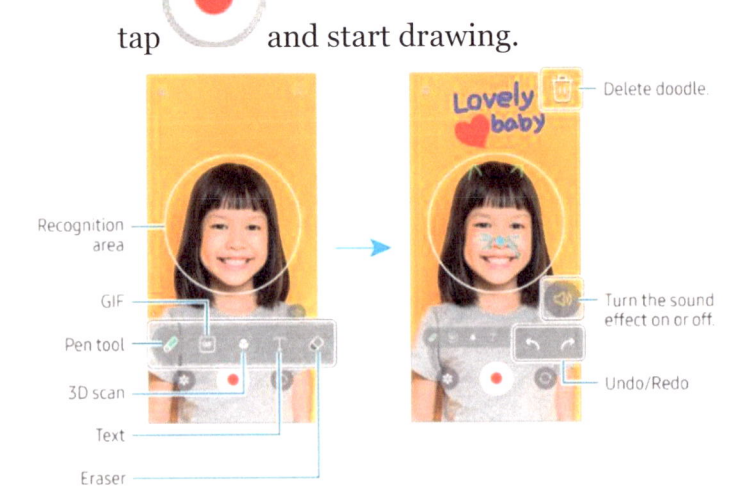

- To record a video, tap ⬤.
- To end the video recording, tap. The video is available for viewing and sharing in the Gallery.

BIXBY

Bixby is a user interface designed to make using your device easier. You can text Bixby or have a conversation. Bixby will provide the information you desire or start a feature you request.

Launching Bixby

To start Bixby, press and hold the Side button. It will show the Bixby intro page. The Bixby screen will show up once you choose the language to use with Bixby, log into your Samsung account, and finish the setup by following the on-screen directions.

Making use of Bixby

Say anything you want to Bixby while holding down the Side button. Alternatively, state what you want and the wake-up word. Say, for instance, "How's the weather today?" while holding down the Side button. The screen will display the weather data. You can carry on a

discussion with Bixby without tapping or hitting the Side button if it asks you a question.

In case the Bixby app icon is not shown on the Apps screen, you may activate it by opening Settings, selecting **Advanced features**

→ **Bixby**, and then tapping the Show Bixby on Apps screen option.

Using your voice to wake Bixby

Saying "Hi, Bixby" or "Bixby" will initiate a conversation with Bixby. To get Bixby to respond to your voice, register your voice.

- Tap ⚙ → Voice wake-up after launching the Bixby app.
- To activate it, tap the switch. 3. Under Wake-up phrase, pick your preferred wake-up phrase.
- To activate it, tap the Respond to my voice switch.
- To finish the setup, adhere to the on-screen directions. You can now initiate a chat by saying the wake-up phrase.

BIXBY VISION

Bixby Vision is a service that uses picture recognition to offer a number of functionalities. By identifying objects, Bixby Vision can be used to find information. Make use of all the helpful Bixby Vision features. Depending on the image size, format, or resolution, this feature might not work or you might not obtain the right search results. Samsung is not liable for the product details that Bixby Vision provides.

Bixby Vision can be launched via one of these techniques.

- Select BIXBY VISION from the list of shooting modes in the Camera app by tapping MORE.
- Choose an image in the Gallery app, then tap ⦿. Touch and hold an image in the Samsung Internet app, then select Search with Bixby Vision.

- Launch the Bixby Vision app if you added its icon to the Apps screen.

Making Use of Bixby Vision

1. Start the Bixby Vision app.

2. Decide whatever feature you wish to utilize.

- **TRANSLATE**: Identify and translate text from pictures or documents.
- **TEXT**: Identify and extract text from pictures or documents.
- **DISCOVER**: Look for pictures of the identified object online along with relevant details. Depending on the area or

carrier, different features and search results may be accessible.

SAMSUNG INTERNET

Look up information online and save your favorite websites to your bookmarks for easy access.

1. Launch the Internet application.

2. Tap **GO** after entering a term or web address. Swipe the screen slightly downward if the toolbar is not visible. Tap or swipe the address field to the left or right to change tabs.

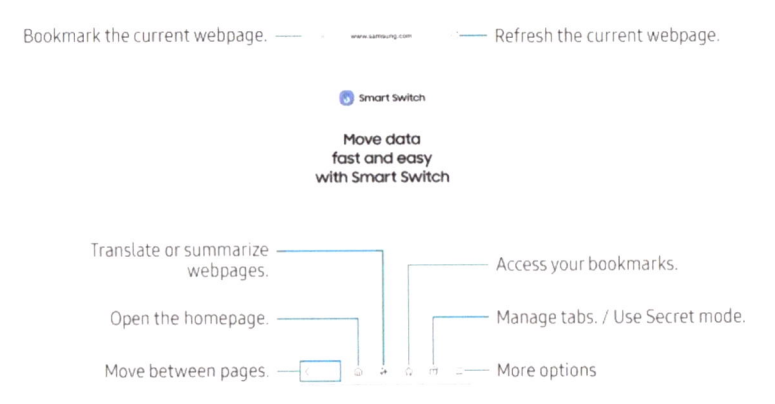

Bookmark the current webpage. — www.samsung.com — Refresh the current webpage.

Move data fast and easy with Smart Switch

Translate or summarize webpages. — Access your bookmarks.
Open the homepage. — Manage tabs. / Use Secret mode.
Move between pages. — More options

You may stop people from viewing your bookmarks, saved pages, browsing history, and search history by creating a password for Secret mode.

Activate Secret mode with a single tap.

After turning it on by tapping the Lock Secret mode button, select Start and then enter a password to access Secret mode. The gadget will

alter the toolbars' color when in secret mode.
Tapping → Turn off Secret mode will turn it off.

SAMSUNG WALLET

Utilize the Samsung Wallet's many practical functions. You may check your boarding cards or tickets, pay for them, use your biometric information to confirm your identification, and more.

Launch the Wallet app, then choose a desired function.

- Depending on the location, this app might not be accessible.
- Depending on the location, certain functionalities might not be accessible.

Configuring the Samsung Wallet

Follow the on-screen directions to finish the initial setup when you launch this application for the first time or when you resume it after doing a data reset.

1. Launch the Wallet app.

2. Read and accept the terms and conditions after logging into your Samsung account.

3. Set up a PIN and fingerprint to be used for payments. This PIN will be needed to validate a number of Samsung Wallet operations, including payment processing and app unlocking.

Make payments

To make payments both online and offline, register your cards with Samsung Pay.

- Drag a picture of a card from the bottom of the screen up. Or launch the Wallet application. Next, choose a card to utilize by swiping left or right on the cards list.
- Enter your payment PIN or scan your fingerprint.

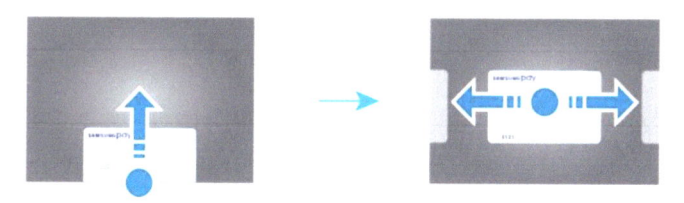

- Touch the card reader on the back of your device. The payment will be processed once the card reader has recognized the card details.

- Your network connection may affect whether or not payments are processed.
- Depending on the card reader, different payment verification methods may be used.

Payment cancellation

By going to the location where you made the payment, you can cancel it. To choose the card you used, swipe left or right on the cards list. To fully cancel your payment, adhere to the on-screen directions.

WI-FI

To connect to a Wi-Fi network and use the internet or other network devices, turn on the Wi-Fi function.

Establishing a Wi-Fi network connection

- To activate Wi-Fi, select **Connections** → **Wi-Fi** from the Settings app, then hit the switch.
- From the list of Wi-Fi networks, pick one. Passwords are required for networks that have a lock icon.

Direct Wi-Fi

Wi-Fi Direct eliminates the need for an access point by connecting devices straight over a Wi-Fi network.

- To activate Wi-Fi, select **Connections** → **Wi-Fi** from the Settings app, then hit the switch.
- Press ⋮ → **Wi-Fi Direct**. The gadgets that were found are listed. Turn on the Wi-Fi Direct feature of the device you wish to connect to if it is not on the list.
- Choose a device to attach to. When the other device accepts the Wi-Fi Direct connection request, the two devices will be linked.
- Choose the device to disconnect from the list to terminate the connection.

BLUETOOTH

To share media files or data with other Bluetooth-enabled devices, use Bluetooth.

Bluetooth data transfer is supported by many apps. Data like contacts or media files can be shared with other Bluetooth-enabled devices. Here are some examples of how to send a photograph to a different device.

- Choose an image by opening the Gallery app.

- Select a device to receive the image by tapping → **Bluetooth**. Turn on the visibility feature for the device you wish to pair with if it isn't on the list.

- Accept the other device's request to connect over Bluetooth.

CONTACTLESS AND NFC PAYMENTS

Near field communications tags (NFC) that hold product information can be read with your phone. After downloading the necessary apps, you can also utilize this function to pay.

- To enable NFC and contactless payments, select **Connections** from the Settings app, then hit the switch.
- On the rear of your device, position the NFC antenna region close to an NFC tag. The tag's information is displayed.

Note: Make sure the screen of the smartphone is unlocked and switched on. If not, the gadget won't be able to scan NFC tags or get data.

Using the NFC function to make payments

You must sign up for a mobile payment provider before you can utilize the NFC function to make payments.

- To enable NFC and contactless payments, select **Connections** from the Settings app, then hit the switch.
- To use the NFC card reader, touch the NFC antenna region on the rear of your device. Open the Settings screen, select **Connections**, then press **NFC and contactless payments**. Inside here, hit **Contactless payments** > **Payment**, and then pick an app to set as the default payment app.

MOBILE HOTSPOT

To share your phone's mobile data connection with other devices, use it as a mobile hotspot.

- Select **Connections**, then press **Mobile Hotspot and Tethering**. Next, hit **Mobile Hotspot** from the Settings app.
- To activate it, tap the switch. Among other things, you can modify the network name and password. The status bar displays the icon .

- Look for and choose your phone from the list of Wi-Fi networks on the screen of the other device. As an alternative, use the other device to scan the QR code after tapping it on the Mobile Hotspot interface.

FACIAL RECOGNITION

The gadget can be configured to recognize your face and unlock the screen.

When you first turn on the device and utilize your face as a screen lock method, your face cannot be used to unlock the screen. You must use the pattern, PIN, or password you created when registering the face to unlock the screen in order to use the device.

Add facial recognition

Registering your face indoors and away from direct sunshine will improve the process.

- Select **Security and privacy → Biometrics → Face recognition** from the Settings app.
- Tap **Continue** after reading the instructions displayed on the screen.

- Configure a screen lock mechanism.
- Place your face within the screen's frame. Your face will be scanned by the camera.

Using your face to unlock the screen

Instead of utilizing a pattern, PIN, or password, you can use your face to unlock the screen.

- Select **Security and privacy → Biometrics → Face recognition** from the Settings app.
- Use the default screen lock technique to unlock the screen.
- To activate it, tap the Face unlock switch.
- Examine the screen on the locked screen. You can unlock the screen without utilizing any extra screen lock techniques once your face has been identified. Make use of the default screen lock technique if your face is not detected.

Deleting your registered facial data

You have the option to remove your registered face data.

- Select **Security and privacy → Biometrics → Face recognition** from the Settings app.
- Use the default screen lock technique to unlock the screen.

- To remove facial data, tap **Remove** > **Remove. All** associated features will be disabled upon deletion of the registered face.

FINGERPRINT RECOGNITION

Your fingerprint information must be registered and saved on your device for fingerprint recognition to work. The availability of this feature may vary based on the model or carrier. Fingerprint identification improves your device's security by utilizing each fingerprint's distinct qualities. There is very little chance that the fingerprint sensor will mistake two distinct fingerprints. Rarely, though, a sensor may identify two distinct fingerprints as same if they are strikingly similar.

Fingerprint registration

To register your fingerprint, select **Security and privacy → Biometrics → Fingerprints** from the Settings app, then adhere to the on-screen directions.

Unlock screen with fingerprints

Instead of utilizing a pattern, PIN, or password, you can use your fingerprint to unlock the screen.

- Select **Security and privacy → Biometrics → Fingerprints** from the Settings app.
- Use the default screen lock technique to unlock the screen.
- To activate it, tap the fingerprint unlock switch.
- Put your finger on the fingerprint identification sensor on the locked screen, then scan your fingerprint.

Removing fingerprints that have been registered

Registered fingerprints can be removed.

- Select **Security and privacy → Biometrics → Fingerprints** from the Settings app.
- Use the default screen lock technique to unlock the screen.
- Tap **Remove** after selecting a fingerprint to remove.

ABOUT THE AUTHOR

Douglas C. McNally is a skilled tech writer who has worked in the field for more than 20 years. He knows a lot about different kinds of consumer technology, from laptops and other new gadgets to smartphones like the iPhone and Samsung Galaxy series.

Douglas has a lot of knowledge about technology, which lets him break down complex ideas into simple guides that regular people can follow. He now resides in Pennsylvania and keeps researching the newest tech trends while writing to share what he has learned.

INDEX

A

Adding contacts ...46
Air actions 32, 33, 34
Air command 30, 34, 36, 37, 38, 40, 42
apps screen........... 14
AR Doodle 82
AR Emoji Stickers 79, 80
AR Zone... 76, 77, 79, 80, 82
auto framing.........63

B

Battery 7
Bixby Vision .. 36, 41, 42, 85, 86
Blocking phone numbers............45

C

Camera 28, 33, 51, 76, 86
camera button 52, 53, 55
Capturing images . 51
Charging 7, 31
close-up images....59

Contactless and NFC payments 94
Contacts...10, 46, 47, 48, 78

D

Deleting contacts. 48
Dual rec mode 63

E

Edge panel 18
Emoji Studio by AR 77
Exposure (AE) and focus (AF) locking 54

F

Facial recognition 96
filters.............. 60, 66
Fingerprint recognition....... 98
Food mode............ 71

G

Gallery 21, 22, 23, 28, 38, 40, 41, 60, 62, 66, 69, 74, 75, 76, 83, 86, 93

101

Generative edit 75

H

Hard Buttons 5
home screen.... 14, 17
Hyperlapse mode. 73

I

Image remastering
 76
Importing contacts
 46
international call . 44

K

keyboard .. 25, 26, 27

M

Messages.48, 49, 50, 80
Mobile Hotspot... 95, 96

N

Night mode 70
Notification panel.19

P

Panorama mode ...71
Pasting and copying
 27
phone calls 44

picture-in-picture63, 65
playback media 21
Portrait mode /
 Portrait video
 mode................. 67
Pro video mode 68

Q

quick settings panel
 19

R

Receive Calls 45

S

S Pen . 24, 30, 31, 32, 33, 34, 35, 36, 37, 41, 42, 43
Samsung account 10, 37, 39, 46, 78, 84, 90
Samsung Internet
 .... 86, 88
Samsung Wallet ...90
Scanning text or
 documents........60
screen record 21
Screen write ...36, 40
screenshot . 6, 21, 22, 23, 41
Selfie-taking.........59
Send messages 49

Side button . 6, 51, 84
Single take mode ..66
Slow motion Mode
72
Smart select... 36, 38
Soft-buttons 13

T

text.....20, 25, 26, 27, 28, 36, 37, 41, 42, 43, 60, 61, 84, 86
Translate 36, 42

V

Video mode...........61
Video stabilization62
Viewing pictures...74

W

Wi-Fi........ 92, 93, 96
Wireless power
 sharing 8

Z

zoom features 53

Made in the USA
Columbia, SC
09 May 2025